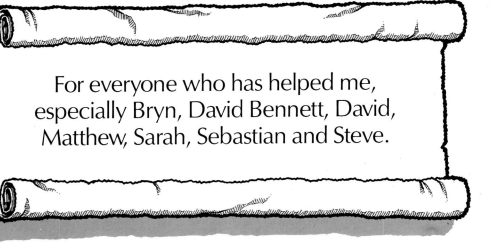

For everyone who has helped me, especially Bryn, David Bennett, David, Matthew, Sarah, Sebastian and Steve.

Copyright © 1989 by Martin Handford

Checklist compiled by Stuart Cooper

First Edition

ISBN 0-316-34282-3

Library of Congress Catolog Card No. 89-84525

10   9   8   7

PRINTED AND BOUND BY L.E.G.O., IN VICENZA ITALY

THE GREAT WALDO SEARCH

MARTIN HANDFORD

Little, Brown and Company
Boston   Toronto   London

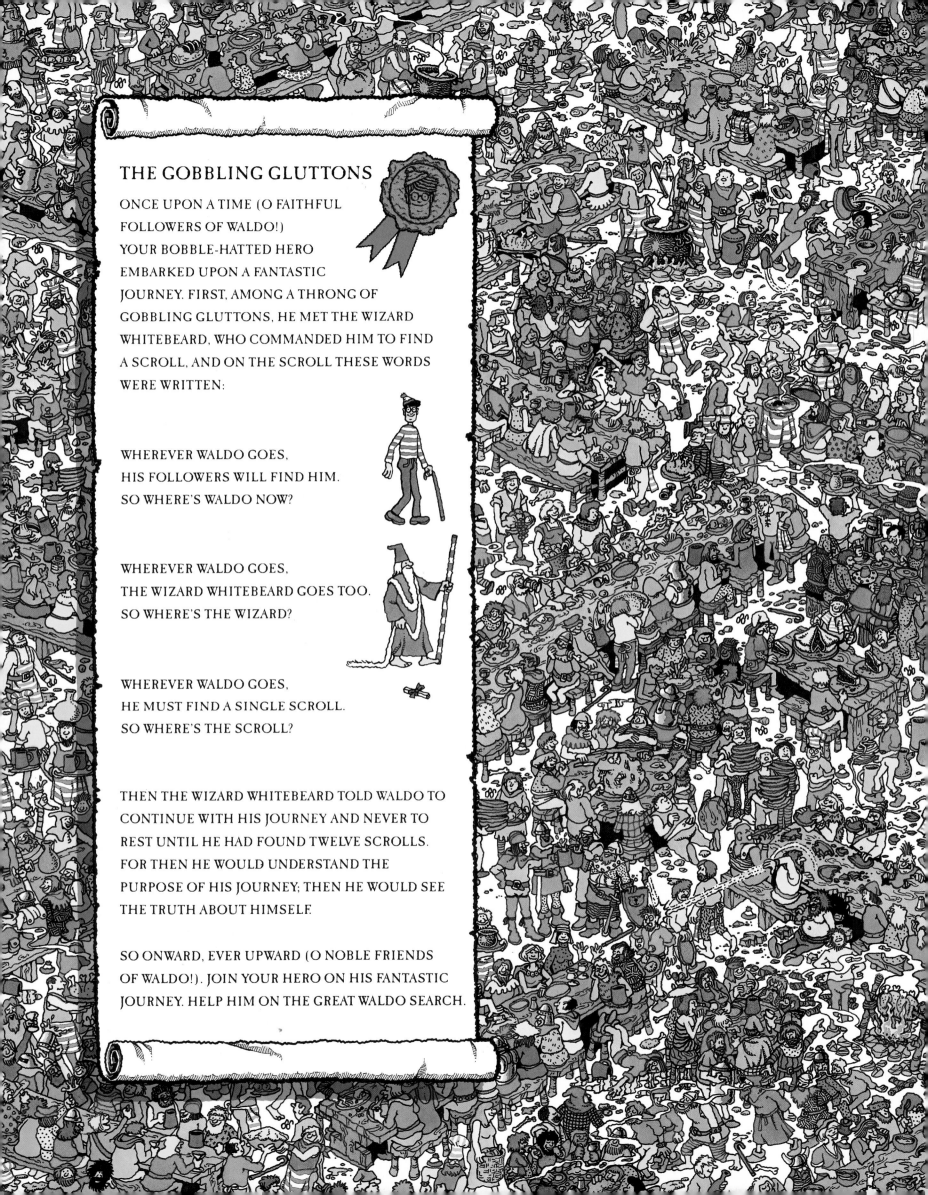

THE GOBBLING GLUTTONS

ONCE UPON A TIME (O FAITHFUL
FOLLOWERS OF WALDO!)
YOUR BOBBLE-HATTED HERO
EMBARKED UPON A FANTASTIC
JOURNEY. FIRST, AMONG A THRONG OF
GOBBLING GLUTTONS, HE MET THE WIZARD
WHITEBEARD, WHO COMMANDED HIM TO FIND
A SCROLL, AND ON THE SCROLL THESE WORDS
WERE WRITTEN:

WHEREVER WALDO GOES,
HIS FOLLOWERS WILL FIND HIM.
SO WHERE'S WALDO NOW?

WHEREVER WALDO GOES,
THE WIZARD WHITEBEARD GOES TOO.
SO WHERE'S THE WIZARD?

WHEREVER WALDO GOES,
HE MUST FIND A SINGLE SCROLL.
SO WHERE'S THE SCROLL?

THEN THE WIZARD WHITEBEARD TOLD WALDO TO
CONTINUE WITH HIS JOURNEY AND NEVER TO
REST UNTIL HE HAD FOUND TWELVE SCROLLS.
FOR THEN HE WOULD UNDERSTAND THE
PURPOSE OF HIS JOURNEY; THEN HE WOULD SEE
THE TRUTH ABOUT HIMSELF.

SO ONWARD, EVER UPWARD (O NOBLE FRIENDS
OF WALDO!). JOIN YOUR HERO ON HIS FANTASTIC
JOURNEY. HELP HIM ON THE GREAT WALDO SEARCH.

THE BATTLING MONKS

THEN WALDO AND THE WIZARD WHITEBEARD CAME TO THE PLACE WHERE THE INVISIBLE MONKS OF FIRE FOUGHT THE MONKS OF WATER. AND AS WALDO SEARCHED FOR THE SECOND SCROLL, HE SAW THAT MANY WALDOS HAD BEEN THIS WAY BEFORE. FIND WALDO. HELP HIM FIND THE SCROLL. THEN CONTINUE ON THE JOURNEY.

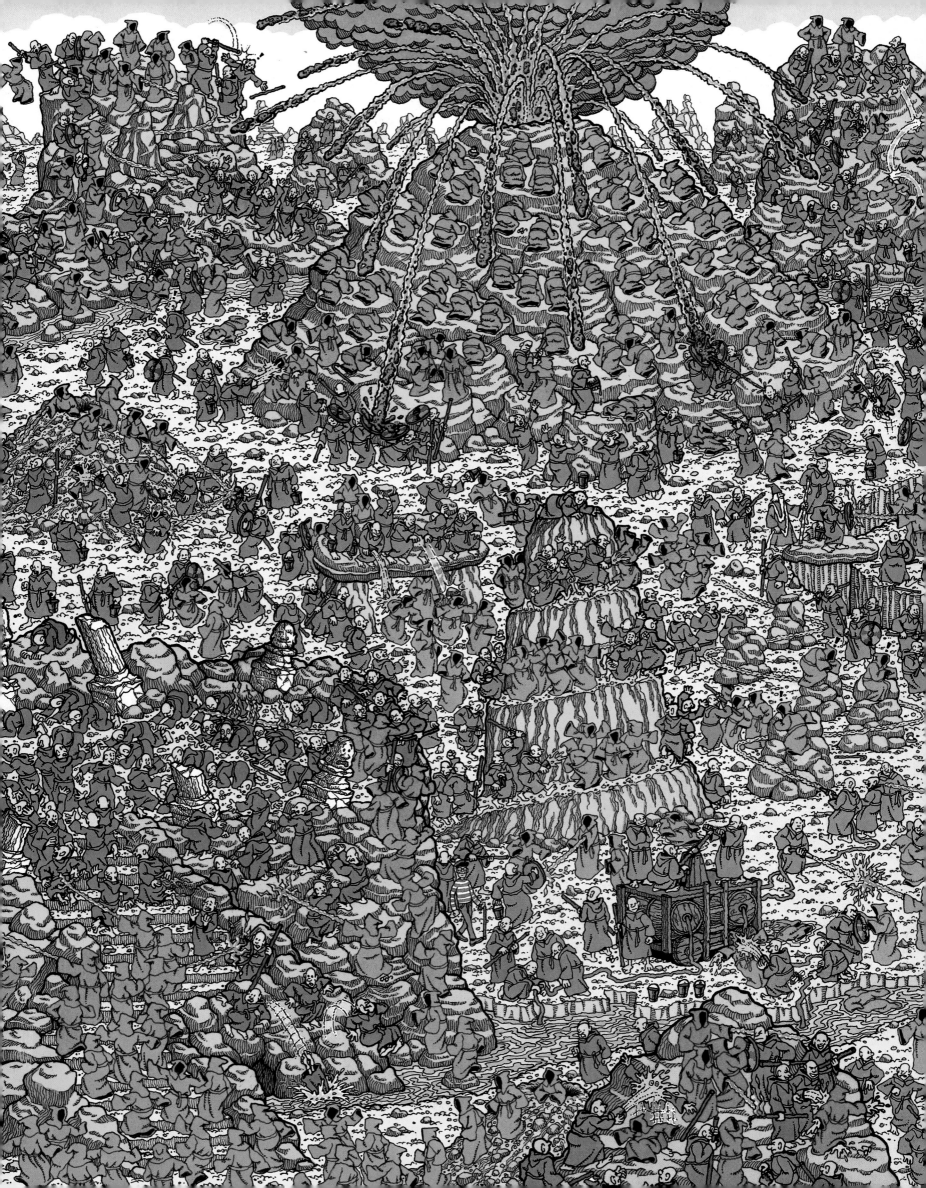

THE CARPET FLYERS

WALDO AND THE WIZARD WHITEBEARD
CAME TO THE LAND OF THE CARPET FLYERS,
WHERE MANY WALDOS HAD BEEN BEFORE.
AND WALDO SAW THAT THERE WERE MANY
CARPETS IN THE SKY AND MANY RED BIRDS.
(HOW MANY, O BRAINY BIRD WATCHERS?)
WHERE'S WALDO? FIND THE THIRD SCROLL AND CONTINUE
ON THE GREAT WALDO SEARCH.

THE GREAT BALL-GAME PLAYERS

THEN WALDO AND THE WIZARD WHITEBEARD CAME TO THE PLAYING FIELD OF THE GREAT BALL GAME, WHERE MANY WALDOS HAD BEEN BEFORE. AND WALDO SAW THAT FOUR TEAMS WERE PLAYING AGAINST EACH OTHER. (BUT WAS ANYONE WINNING? WHAT WAS THE SCORE? CAN YOU WORK OUT THE RULES?) THEN WALDO FOUND THE FOURTH SCROLL AND CONTINUED WITH HIS JOURNEY.

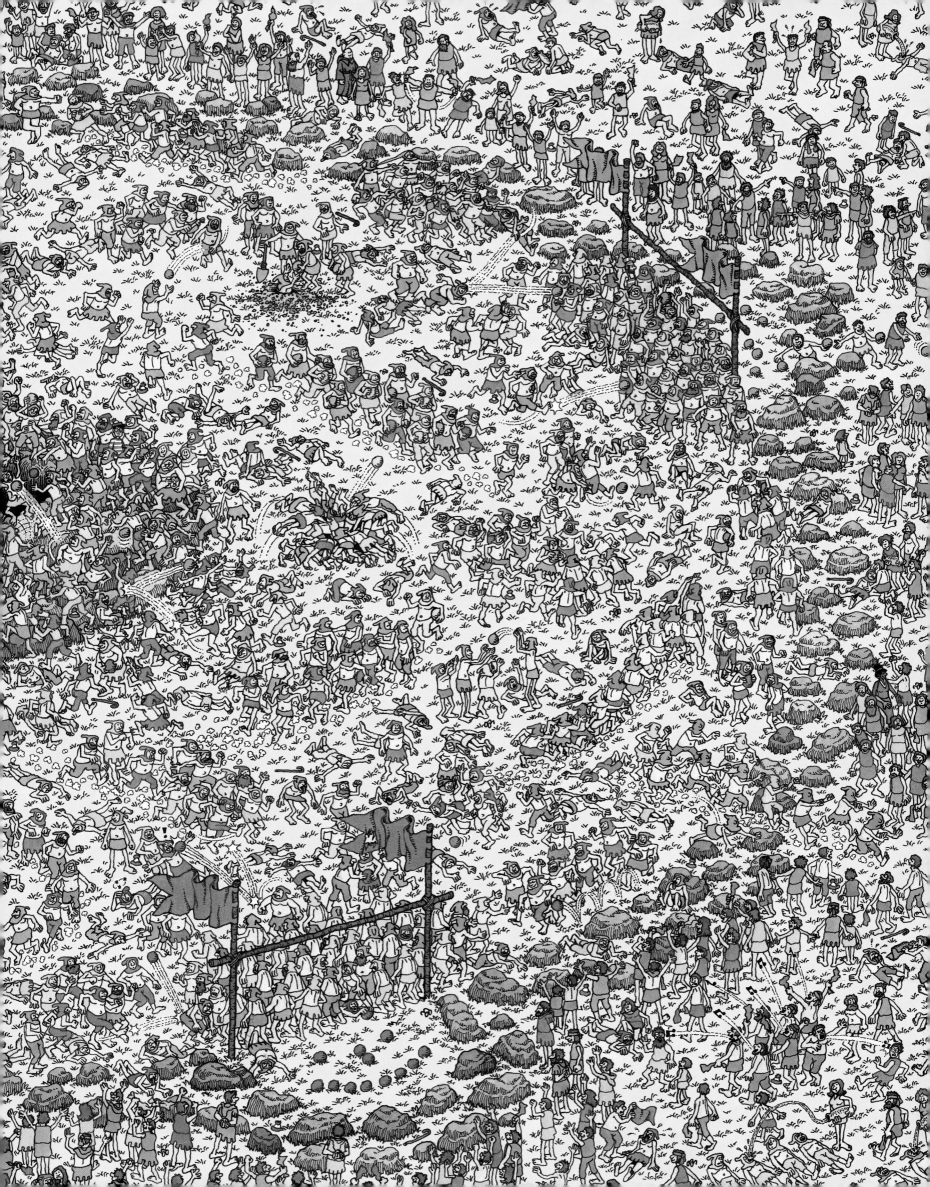

THE FEROCIOUS RED DWARVES

WALDO AND THE WIZARD WHITEBEARD CAME AMONG THE FEROCIOUS RED DWARVES, WHERE MANY WALDOS HAD BEEN BEFORE. THE DWARVES WERE ATTACKING THE MANY-COLORED SPEARMEN, CAUSING MIGHTY MAYHEM AND HORRID HAVOC. AND WALDO FOUND THE FIFTH SCROLL AND CONTINUED ON THE GREAT WALDO SEARCH.

THE NASTY NASTIES

THEN WALDO AND THE WIZARD WHITEBEARD CAME TO THE CASTLE OF THE NASTY NASTIES, WHERE MANY WALDOS HAD BEEN BEFORE. AND WHEREVER WALDO WALKED, THERE WAS A FEARFUL CLATTERING OF BONES, A FIENDISH CACKLING OF WITCHES, A FOUL SLURPING OF FILTHY FOOD. AND WALDO FOUND THE SIXTH SCROLL AS QUICKLY AS HE COULD AND CONTINUED WITH HIS JOURNEY.

THE FIGHTING FORESTERS

WALDO AND THE WIZARD WHITEBEARD CAME
AMONG THE FIGHTING FORESTERS, WHERE MANY
WALDOS HAD BEEN BEFORE. IN THEIR BATTLE
WITH THE EVIL KNIGHTS, THE FOREST WOMEN WERE
AIDED BY THE ANIMALS, BY THE LIVING MUD — EVEN BY THE
TREES THEMSELVES. AND WALDO FOUND THE SEVENTH SCROLL
AND CONTINUED ON THE GREAT WALDO SEARCH.

THE DEEP-SEA DIVERS

THEN WALDO AND THE WIZARD WHITEBEARD CAME
TO THE WATERY WORLD OF THE DEEP-SEA DIVERS,
WHERE MANY WALDOS HAD BEEN BEFORE.
WALDO SEARCHED FOR THE EIGHTH SCROLL AMONG
THE MONSTERS OF THE DEEP, AMONG THE MERMAIDS,
FISHERMEN, AND FISH. FIND WALDO. FIND THE SCROLL
AND CONTINUE ON THE JOURNEY.

THE KNIGHTS OF THE MAGIC FLAG

WALDO AND THE WIZARD WHITEBEARD CAME TO A PLACE MORE CROWDED THAN ANY WALDO HAD SEEN BEFORE. TWO ARMIES WITH MANY MAGIC FLAGS WERE LOCKED IN COMBAT, AND WALDO SAW THAT MANY WALDOS HAD BEEN THIS WAY BEFORE. FIND WALDO. FIND THE NINTH SCROLL AND CONTINUE ON THE GREAT WALDO SEARCH.

THE UNFRIENDLY GIANTS

THEN WALDO AND THE WIZARD WHITEBEARD CAME
TO THE LAND OF THE UNFRIENDLY GIANTS,
WHERE MANY WALDOS HAD BEEN BEFORE.
WALDO SAW THAT THE GIANTS WERE HORRIDLY
HARASSING THE LITTLE PEOPLE. AND WHEN HE FOUND THE
TENTH SCROLL, IT WAS TIME TO CONTINUE HIS JOURNEY.

THE UNDERGROUND HUNTERS

WALDO AND THE WIZARD WHITEBEARD CAME AMONG THE UNDERGROUND HUNTERS, WHERE MANY WALDOS HAD BEEN BEFORE. AND THERE WAS MUCH MENACE IN THIS PLACE — A MULTITUDE OF MALEVOLENT MONSTERS. HELP WALDO FIND THE ELEVENTH SCROLL AND CONTINUE ON HIS JOURNEY.

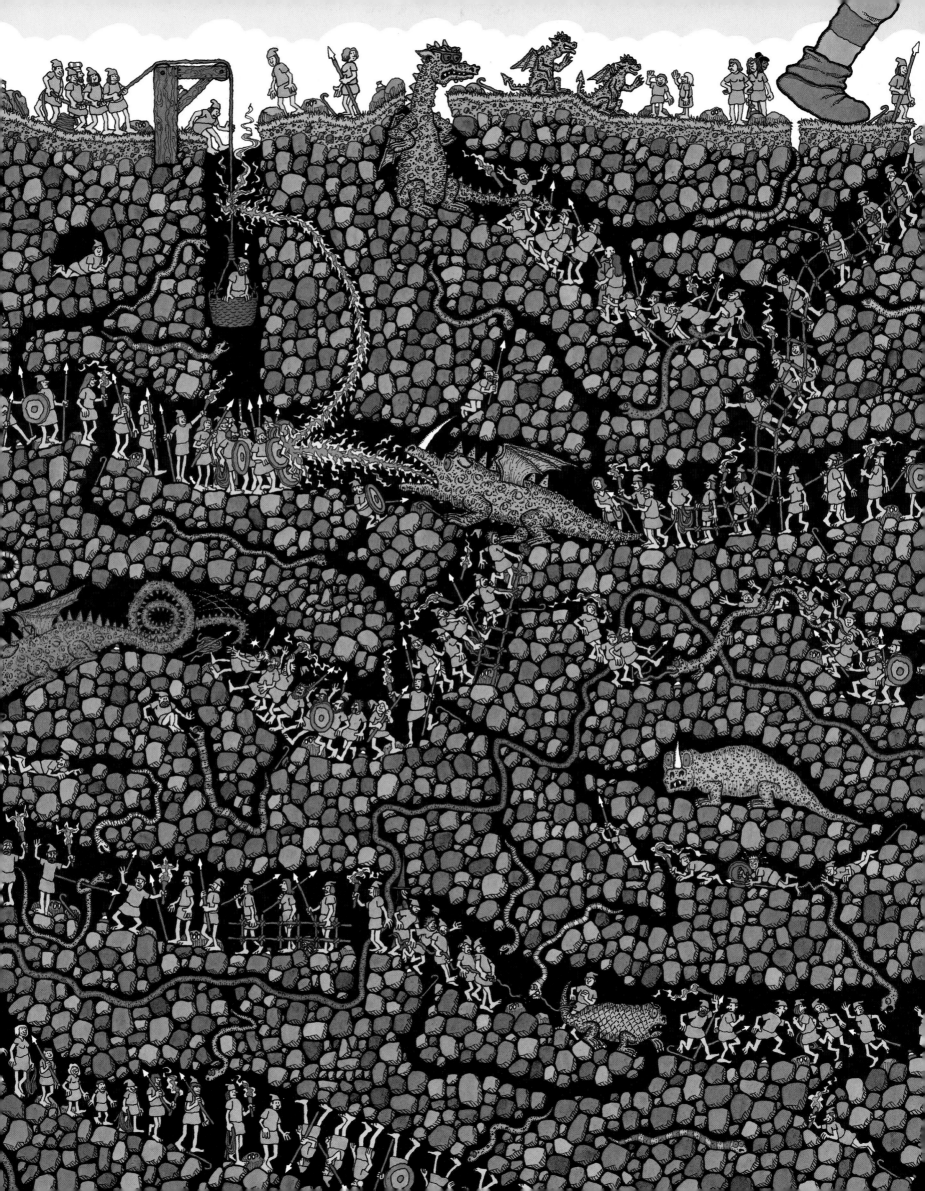

THE LAND OF WALDOS

FINALLY WALDO FOUND THE TWELFTH SCROLL AND SAW THE TRUTH ABOUT HIMSELF. HE WAS JUST ONE WALDO AMONG MANY. HE SAW, TOO, THAT WALDOS OFTEN LOSE THINGS, FOR HE HIMSELF HAD LOST ONE SHOE. AS HE LOOKED FOR HIS SHOE, HE DISCOVERED THAT THE WIZARD WHITEBEARD WAS NOT HIS ONLY FELLOW TRAVELER. THERE WERE NOW ELEVEN OTHERS — ONE FROM EVERY PLACE HE HAD BEEN TO — THEY HAD JOINED HIM ONE BY ONE ALONG THE WAY. SO NOW (O LOYAL FOLLOWERS OF WALDO!) FIND THE REAL WALDO AND HELP HIM FIND HIS MISSING SHOE. AND THERE, IN THE LAND OF WALDOS, MAY WALDO LIVE HAPPILY EVER AFTER.

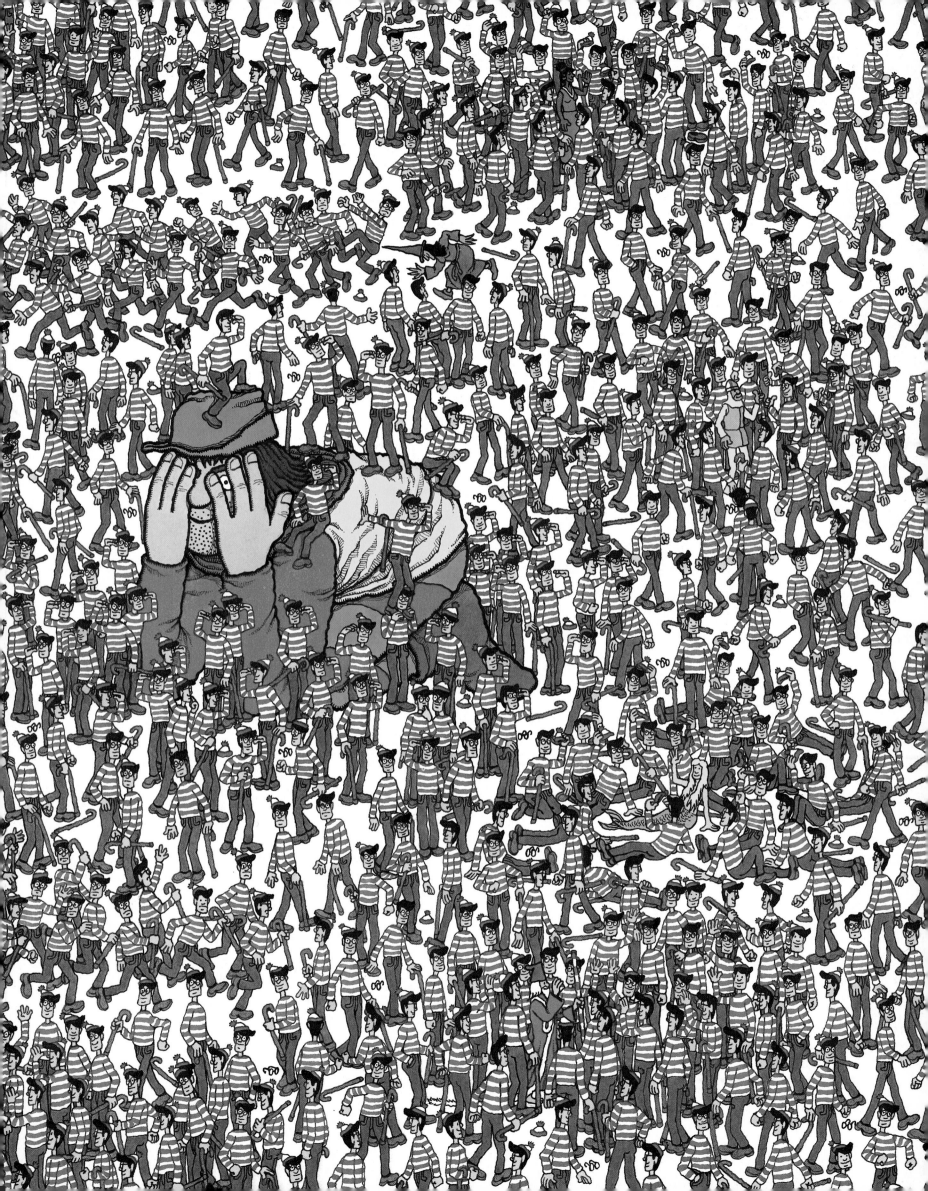

THE GREAT WALDO SEARCH CHECKLIST
Hundreds more things for Waldo followers to look for!

THE GOBBLING GLUTTONS
- A strong waiter and a weak one
- Long-distance smells
- Unequal portions of pie
- A man who has had too much to drink
- People who are going the wrong way
- Very tough dishes
- An upside-down dish
- A very hot dinner
- Knights drinking through straws
- A clever drink-pourer
- Giant sausages
- A custard fight
- An overloaded seat
- Beard-flavored soup
- Men pulling legs
- A painful spillage
- A poke in the eye
- A man tied up in spaghetti
- A knock-out dish
- A man who has eaten too much
- A tall diner eating a tall dish
- An exploding pie
- A man in the soup
- A smell travelling through two people

THE CARPET FLYERS
- Two carpets on collision course
- An overweight flyer
- A pedestrian crossing
- A carpet pin-up
- Three hangers-on
- Flying hitch-hikers
- An unsatisfied customer
- A used carpet salesman
- A topsy-turvy tower
- A spiky crash
- Carpet cops and robbers
- A passing fruit thief
- Upside-down flyers
- A carpet repair shop
- Popular male and female flyers
- A flying tower
- A stair carpet
- Flying highwaymen
- Rich and poor flyers
- A carpet-breakdown rescue service
- Carpets flying on carpet flyers
- A carpet traffic policeman
- A flying carpet without a flyer

THE BATTLING MONKS
- Two fire engines
- Hot-footed monks
- A bridge made of monks
- A smart aleck monk
- A diving monk
- A scared statue
- Fire meeting water
- A snaking jet of water
- Chasers being chased
- A smug statue
- A snaking jet of flame
- A five-way wash-out
- A burning bridge
- Seven burning backsides
- Monks worshipping the Flowing Bucket of Water
- Monks shielding themselves from lava
- Thirteen trapped and extremely worried monks
- A monk seeing an oncoming jet of flame
- Monks worshipping the Mighty Erupting Volcano
- A very worried monk confronted by two opponents
- A burning hose
- Monks and lava pouring out of a volcano
- A chain of water
- Two monks accidentally attacking their brothers

THE GREAT BALL-GAME PLAYERS
- A three-way drink
- A row of hand-held banners
- A chase that goes round in circles
- A spectator surrounded by three rival supporters
- Players who can't see where they are going
- Two tall players versus short ones
- Seven awful singers
- A face made of balls
- Players who are digging for victory
- A face about to hit a fist
- A shot that breaks the woodwork
- A mob chasing a player backwards
- A player chasing a mob
- Players pulling each others' hoods
- A flag with a hole in it
- A mob of players all holding balls
- A player heading a ball
- A player tripping over a rock
- A player punching a ball
- A spectator accidentally hitting two others
- A player poking his tongue out at a mob
- A mouth pulled open by a beard
- A backside shot

THE FEROCIOUS RED DWARVES
- A spear-breaking slingshot
- Two punches causing chain reactions
- Fat and thin spears and spearmen
- A spearman being knocked through a flag
- A collar made out of a shield
- A prison made of spears
- Tangled spears
- A devious disarmer
- Dwarves disguised as spearmen
- A stick-up machine
- A spearman trapped by his battle dress
- A sneaky spear-bender
- An axe-head causing headaches
- A dwarf who is on the wrong side
- Dangerous target practice
- Opponents charging through each other
- A spearman running away from a spear
- A slingshot causing a chain reaction
- A sword cutting through a shield
- A spear hitting a spearman's shield
- A dwarf hiding up a spear
- Spearmen who have jumped out of their clothes
- A spear knocking off a dwarf's helmet

THE NASTY NASTIES
- A vampire who is scared of ghosts
- Two vampire bears
- Vampires drinking through straws
- Gargoyle lovers
- An upside-down torture
- A baseball bat
- Three wolfmen
- A mummy who is coming undone
- A vampire mirror test
- A frightened skeleton
- Dog, cat and mouse doorways
- Courting cats
- A ghoulish game of skittles
- A gargoyle being poked in the eye
- An upside-down gargoyle
- Ghoulish flight controllers
- Three witches flying backwards
- A witch losing her broomstick
- A broomstick flying a witch
- A ticklish torture
- A vampire about to get the chop
- A ghost train
- A vampire who doesn't fit his coffin
- A three-eyed, hooded torturer